T0196996

Invoking Reality

Invoking Reality

Moral and Ethical Teachings of Zen

John Daido Loori

Shambhala
Boston & London
2007

Shambhala Publications, Inc.
Horticultural Hall
300 Massachusetts Avenue
Boston, Massachusetts 02115
www.shambhala.com

Photo credits: frontispiece, p. 93: Robert Aichinger;
pp. x, 83: Cameron Broadhurst; p. 8: John Wisbey;
pp. 16, 58, 75: National Buddhist Archive;
p. 28: Chris Potter; p. 36: Carol Kyoryu Dysinger;
pp. 48, 67: Hillary March.

Printed in the United States of America

♾ This edition is printed on acid-free paper that meets the
American National Standards Institute z39.48 Standard.

♻ Shambhala Publications makes every effort to print on recycled
paper. For more information please visit www.shambhala.com.

Distributed in the United States by Penguin Random House LLC
and in Canada by Random House of Canada Ltd

Library of Congress Cataloging-in-Publication Data
Loori, John Daido.
Invoking reality: moral and ethical teachings of Zen /
John Daido Loori.
p. cm.
Originally published: Boston: Dharma Communications, 1998.
ISBN 978-1-59030-459-4 (pbk.: alk. paper)
1. Religious life—Zen Buddhism. 2. Zen
Buddhism—Discipline. 3. Buddhist ethics. I. Title.
BQ9286.L664   2007
294.3′5—dc22
2006052314

Contents

Invoking Reality

The Moral and Ethical Teachings of Zen

When Zen arrived and began to take root in this country, there arose a misconception about the role of morality and ethics in the practice of the Buddhadharma. Statements that Zen was beyond morality or that Zen was amoral were made by distinguished writers on Buddhism, and people assumed that this was correct. Yet nothing can be further from the truth. Enlightenment and morality are one. Enlightenment without morality is not true enlightenment. Morality without enlightenment is not complete morality. Zen is not beyond morality, but a practice that takes place within the world, based on moral and ethical teachings. Those moral and ethical teachings have been handed down with the mind-to-mind transmission from generation to generation.

The Buddhist precepts form one of the most vital areas of spiritual practice. In essence, the precepts are a definition of the life of a Buddha, of how a Buddha functions in the world. They are how enlightened beings live their lives, relate to other human beings, make moral and ethical decisions, manifest wisdom and compassion in everyday life. The precepts provide a way to see how the moral and ethical teachings in Buddhism can come to life in the workplace, in relationships, in government, business, and ecology.

The first three precepts are vows to take refuge in the Three Treasures—the Buddha, the Dharma, and the Sangha. Buddha is the historical Buddha, but at the same time Buddha is each being, each creation. Dharma is the teaching of the Buddha, but at the same time Dharma is the whole phenomenal universe. And Sangha is the community of practitioners of the Buddha's Dharma, but at the same time Sangha is all sentient beings, animate and inanimate.

The Three Pure Precepts are: "not creating evil," "practicing good," and "actualizing good for others." The Pure Precepts define the harmony, the natural order, of things. If we eschew evil, practice good, and actualize good for others, we are in harmony with the natural order of all things.

Of course, it is one thing to acknowledge the Three Pure Precepts, but how can we practice them? How can we not create evil? How can we practice good? How can we actualize good for others? The way to do that is shown in the Ten Grave Precepts, which reveal the functioning of the Three Pure Precepts. The Ten Grave Precepts are: (1) Affirm life; do not kill, (2) Be giving; do not steal, (3) Honor the body; do not misuse sexuality, (4) Manifest truth; do not lie, (5) Proceed clearly; do not cloud the mind, (6) See the perfection; do not speak of others' errors and faults, (7) Realize self and other as one; do not elevate the self and blame others, (8) Give generously; do not be withholding, (9) Actualize harmony; do not be angry, (10) Experience the intimacy of things; do not defile the Three Treasures.

The Sixteen Precepts—taking refuge in the Three Treasures, the Three Pure Precepts, and the Ten Grave Precepts—are not fixed rules of action or a code for moral behavior. They allow for changes in circumstances: for adjusting to the time, the particular place, your position, and the degree of action necessary in any given situation. When we don't hold on to an idea of ourselves and a particular way we have to react, then we are free to respond openly, with reverence for all the life involved.

When we first begin Zen practice, we use the precepts as a guide for living our life as a Buddha. We want to know how to live in harmony with all beings, and we do not want to put it off until after we get enlightened. So, we practice the precepts. We practice them the same way we practice the breath, or the way we practice a koan. To practice means to do. We do the precepts. Once we are aware of the precepts, we become sensitive to the moments when we break them. When you break a precept, you acknowledge that, take responsibility for it, and come back to the precept again. It's just like when you work with the breath in zazen. You sit down on your cushion and you vow to work with the breath, to be the breath. Within three breaths you find yourself thinking about something else, not being the breath at all. When that happens, you acknowledge it, take responsibility for it, let the thought go, and return to the breath. That is how you practice the breath, and that is how you practice the precepts. That is how you practice your life. Practice is not a process for getting someplace; it is not a process that gets us to enlightenment. Practice is, in itself, enlightenment.

It is one thing to study the precepts, but the real

point of practice is to be the precepts through and through, to manifest them with our lives. The precepts are a sword that kills and a sword that gives life. The sword that kills is the absolute basis of reality, no-self. The sword that gives life is the compassion that comes out of that realization of no-self. The precepts are the sword of the realized mind.

The precepts need to be understood clearly from the literal point of view, from the perspective of compassion and reverence for life, and from the absolute, or "one-mind," point of view. Their richness is wasted if we see them simplistically as a set of rules, a list of "dos and don'ts." They are not meant to bind but to liberate. In fact, they define a life that is unhindered, complete, free. What the precepts do is to bring into consciousness that which is already there.

When one only reads about Buddhism, one can come to the conclusion that Zen is amoral, that it considers itself above morality and does not address itself to ethical teachings. That is the view of a person standing on the sidelines, only involved intellectually. Those who truly embrace this practice cannot help but see the intimacy between the Buddhadharma and a moral and ethical life. It is intrinsic to the teaching itself. The life of the Buddha is the manifestation of compassion, but if we do not engage it, it does nothing. It all depends on us. To stand on the sidelines merely thinking about practice is self-styled Zen. For the teachings to come alive, they have to be lived with the whole body and mind.

I feel that because we put such an emphasis on the precepts, we have a moral obligation to do something about that misconception concerning Zen and morality. There are thousands of Zen practitioners in our country, many thousands who have received the precepts and taken refuge in the Three Treasures but who don't really know what they've done. They have no idea what the precepts mean.

Ask yourself what it means to take refuge in the Three Treasures. What is refuge? What, really, are the Three Treasures? We say, "Buddha, Dharma, and Sangha," but what does that mean? Those are the words. What is the reality of Buddha, of being one with the Buddha, being one with the Dharma, being one with the Sangha? It is not some idea. It is a reality, a state of consciousness, a state of being. It is the state of being in harmony with the moral and ethical teachings.

We live in a time period of considerable moral crisis, with an erosion of values and a fragmentation of meaning prevalent throughout the fabric of the society. The crisis impacts on us personally, as a nation, and as a planet. The injuries that we inflict on each other and on our environment can only be healed by sound moral and ethical commitment. That doesn't mean being puritanical. It doesn't mean being "moralistic." These precepts have a vitality that is unique in the great religions. They are alive, not fixed. They function broadly and deeply, taking into account the intricacies and subtleties of conditions encountered.

There is so much to learn. The precepts are incredibly profound. Don't take them lightly. They are direct. They are subtle. They are bottomless. Please use them. Press up against them. Push them. See where they take you. Make them your own. They are no small thing, by any measure. They nourish, they heal, and they give life to the Buddha.

Atonement

REALIZING RESPONSIBILITY

*All evil karma ever committed by me
 since of old,
Because of my beginningless greed, anger,
 and ignorance,
Born of my body, mouth, and thought,
Now I atone for it all.*

Many rites of passage that take place in the context of Zen practice include the Verse of Atonement near the beginning of the ceremony. The Verse of Atonement, or At-one-ment, creates a pure and unconditioned state of consciousness. It introduces an attitude of mind conducive to entering and engaging a new way of being, a mind receptive and open to transformation.

Engaging the precepts as one's life is a serious matter. When we vow to maintain them, making a commitment to manifest our life with the wisdom and compassion of the Tathagata, we enter a new and different realm. In that passage, the Verse of Atonement establishes a clean slate.

The spiritual search begins when we open our mind and heart, raising to consciousness the inherent possibility of completely realizing this human life. We call it raising the bodhi mind. This raising of the bodhi mind simply means seeing, hearing, feeling, experiencing, and realizing in ways that were not even imagined before. It means opening the doors of perception and awareness.

Usually, out of that transformation and opening emerges practice. And practice is doing. Practice means commitment and action. We are no longer observers standing on the sidelines. We become participants.

With practice—the doing, the commitment, the action—there comes discovery and realization. As a result, the precepts begin to be actualized as our own life. We make conscious, in a very personal way, the identity of the life-stream of the Buddhas and ancestors with the life-stream of all sentient beings. Not the life-stream of the Buddhas and ancestors in identity with our life-stream alone, but the life-stream of the Buddhas and ancestors in identity with all sentient beings, which, of course, includes oneself.

Real atonement takes place only when the bodhi mind has been raised and practice is engaged. When that has happened, we're dealing with a very powerful spiritual magnet that attracts everything into the sphere of practice. Raising the bodhi mind, practice and enlightenment thus become one reality.

All evil karma ever committed by me since of old. Every cause has an effect, and every effect is the next cause. But we should always appreciate the fact that cause and effect are one; they are not two distinct events. Cause does not precede effect, and effect does not follow cause. This is why karma does not move in only one direction. Remarkably it moves backward in time and space as well as forward in time and space. It permeates the ten directions.

Because of my beginningless greed, anger, and ignorance. Greed, anger, and ignorance are the three poisons. They are the basis of evil karma. Transformed, they become the three virtues—compassion, wisdom, and enlightenment, and these qualities are the basis of good karma. They describe a way of being in harmony with the nature of all things.

Born of my body, mouth, and thought. Body, mouth, and thought are the spheres of action where karma is created, both good and evil. What we do with our bodies, what we do with our words, and what we do with our thoughts, all lead to consequences, all establish specific karma. We should appreciate this fact thoroughly.

Body language speaks outwardly and inwardly. When you clench your fists and grit your teeth, you create anger mentally and physically. When you place your hands in the cosmic mudra, you create a state of consciousness that reflects introspection and peace. What we do with our bodies is who we are. It is for that reason that the posture of zazen is so important.

When we bow, we manifest the body karma of the three virtues. When we gassho, we manifest the body karma of the three virtues. It is nearly impossible to communicate the meaning of this in words. Most of it is a process of personal discovery. If you just sit cross-legged and make the cosmic mudra with your hands, you may appreciate how that mudra affects your whole being, how it can turn your attention inward to the deepest aspects of yourself. There are other mudras, some that turn you outward, toward the world, but all of them are about the karma of body.

Words are also karma. What we say has a tremendous impact on our lives and on the world around us. When we vow to attain the Way, we connect with the karma of that vow. In chanting the name of the Buddha, we are one with the Buddha. There is no separation. On the other hand, ''God, give me a Mercedes'' creates an immediate separation. When our words are motivated by compassion and wisdom, they manifest as wisdom and compassion. When our words are motivated by greed, anger, and ignorance, that's what they manifest. When we express goodwill, we create the karma of goodwill. When we express anger, we create the karma of anger.

There is also the illusive karma of thought, which is all too often unrecognized. Thought, in and of itself, has the ability to transform. Actually, transformation can occur in all three spheres, but generally we pay little attention to the cause-and-effect power of thought. We think it is a very personal, invisible process, and that nobody knows about it. But thoughts radiate like signals from a telecommunication satellite. We project what we are thinking in hundreds of ways. What we think touches the world and it touches us.

When thoughts move inward, and these thoughts are thoughts of greed, anger, and ignorance, we end up chewing up our own bodies. We end up destroying ourselves. This happens on both an individual and a collective level. Sometimes it is easy to see this in people's faces; somebody who is fifty years old looks a hundred; somebody who is a hundred years old looks fifty. Why? It is about body, mouth, and thought. It is karma that creates who we are, how we live our lives, how we relate to each other, and how we relate to ourselves. It is that simple and that important.

Now I atone for it all. When at-one-ment takes place with the whole body and mind, you have created a state that is pure and unconditioned. Spiritual realization and moral action are one reality. They are interdependent—just like cause and effect. Enlightenment is not beyond good and evil, as popularized Zen would have us believe. It is rather a way of using one's body and mind and living one's life with a clear and unequivocal moral commitment. Enlightenment is realized and actualized not only in the realm of good and evil but also within all dualities, and is at the same time not stained by those dualities. To realize the Verse of Atonement is to enter the practice of the precepts with the whole body and mind, prepared to make the enlightenment of all Buddhas, past and present, one's true self.

Taking Refuge in the
Three Treasures

When I listen to the precepts, the vows, and the service dedications, when I feel my body in the bows, when I connect with the Buddhas and ancestors in the daily liturgy, I am touched by an incredible sense of gratitude for having the opportunity to hear, experience, and participate in these teachings. I know it is a gift that I will never be able to repay. It makes me wonder how often any of us appreciates how profound Zen practice is. Do we really hear it? Do we sense it? Do we feel it with our bones, right down to the marrow, with every cell in our bodies—or is it just another fling, a dharma fling? It is vitally important to appreciate this life. In one sense, that is what taking refuge in the Three Treasures really is about, appreciating our life, appreciating all life, waking up again and again to that feeling.

People ask, "How can I deepen the teacher-student relationship?" It is like asking, "How can I love you?" Is there a book of instructions on how to love? Does the baby get taught how to love its mother, the flowers, the earth, and the rain? In Zen training we say, "Really put yourself into it," but what does that mean? It means to take refuge and to be protected by the Three Treasures. What are the Three Treasures? We chant, "Being one with the Buddha, being one with the Dharma, being one with the Sangha." Those are the Three Treasures, but what does it mean to "be one with"? This is what we need to see, to realize clearly and personally.

The word we translate as refuge is taken from the Japanese term *kie-ei*. *Kie-ei* consists of two characters. *Kie* means "to unreservedly throw oneself into," no holding back, no way out, no safety net, harness, or rope. That is the way a parent rescues a child who is in danger. The parent does not think about himself or herself. The parent does not hesitate for a second. The second character, *ei*, literally means "to rely upon," in the way that a child leaps into a parent's arms, trusting unequivocally.

Taking Refuge in the Three Treasures

I remember when my children were young. They were able to stand by themselves but couldn't yet walk, and I would stand them up on the dresser and say, "Jump!" They would throw themselves into space, knowing I would be there. They had a complete sense of trust. It was total doing. "Unreservedly throwing oneself into and relying upon" differs from "a shelter or protection from danger or distress"—the more common definition of the word refuge.

Before we can appreciate *kie-ei* we need to appreciate what it is we are relying upon and unreservedly throwing ourselves into—the Buddha, the Dharma, and the Sangha. Usually we understand Buddha to be the historical Buddha. From an inclusive perspective, we say that all beings are Buddha. Also, Buddha is the teacher. We see Dharma as being the teachings of the Buddha, the medicine to heal the sickness, and sometimes it is the ten thousand things. We understand Sangha as the practitioners of the Buddha's Dharma, our companions along the way, and we also understand it as the whole phenomenal universe, all sentient beings.

Then, there is a much deeper way to appreciate these Three Treasures. Perhaps if we appreciate them deeply enough, we will realize what it means to take refuge in the Buddha, the Dharma, and the Sangha;

to vow to save all sentient beings, to put an end to desires, to master the dharmas, and to accomplish the Way. Perhaps we will understand what it means to be one with this unwavering lineage of ancestors who have handed down this dharma from generation to generation, without holding anything back. They gave their lives to it; not three months, six months, a year, five or ten years, but their whole lives. They turned themselves inside out. They renounced every-thing else to make the Way clear. Why? So we can have it, here and now, served to us on a platter. It is ours for the taking. All we have to do is reach out.

What does it mean to reach out? It means to have exhaustively asked the questions: What is Buddha? What is Dharma? What is Sangha? What does it mean to take refuge? What does it mean to vow? What does it mean to be one with? What does it mean to com-mit? What does it mean to have a relationship with a teacher? The answers are all available. Nothing is hidden.

We can find it in books. We can find it in the sutras. We can find it by asking. And, most important, we can find it simply by looking into ourself. Why do we practice? What is it that we seek? What is it that we want? What is it that we are prepared to do to get what we want? Are we willing to practice the edge, take a risk, unreservedly throw ourself into practice? Or are we just being opportunistic and calculating, ready only to skim a little cream off the top to take care of the immediate problems, but not ready to go to the depths?

The Three Treasures can be seen in many different ways. One way of understanding them is as the unified Three Treasures. The Buddha Treasure, from the perspective of the unified Three Treasures, is *anuttara-samyaksambodhi,* perfect enlightenment. No one is without it. It does not increase one bit in Buddhas, nor is it reduced one bit in "ordinary" beings. It is our fundamental nature, the fundamental nature of each and every one of us. It is the essential reality of this great earth and of the universe. It is vast. It is empty. It is without self-nature. The virtues of the dharma of wisdom and liberation emerge from *anuttara-samyaksambodhi.* It is from here that we realize the three bodies of the Buddha—Dharmakaya, Sambhogakaya, and Nirmanakaya.

From the perspective of the unified Three Treasures, the Dharma Treasure is undefiled purity. There is neither a speck of defilement nor a single particle of ego in the Dharma Treasure. The Dharma reaches everywhere. There is nothing outside it. Where could the defilement possibly come from? Dharma embraces everything. It is for that reason it is pure and undefiled.

From the perspective of the unified Three Treasures, the Sangha Treasure is virtue and merit of harmony. What we call harmony is really the fusion of the Buddha Treasure and the Dharma Treasure. Buddha, or fundamental nature, is empty of all characteristics, yet there is an arising of karma, cause and effect, which is dharma nature. There is this arising of causation, or dharma, yet fundamental nature is empty. This vital matter is the life of each one of us.

Another way of looking at the Three Treasures is as the manifested Three Treasures. Direct realization of bodhi is called the Buddha Treasure. Buddha was the first person to realize bodhi. Each generation thereafter has rekindled that realization as personal experience. Enlightened masters opened their eye and transmitted it from generation to generation, from country to country. That is the manifested Buddha Treasure.

The Dharma of the manifested Three Treasures is the Buddha's realization. That realization of the Buddha is at once the realization of all sentient beings, past, present, and future; your life and my life.

The Sangha of the manifested Three Treasures is the practicing of the Buddha's dharma. The moment two people get together and practice—not just to go through the gestures, take the form, use the vernacular, or dress in the clothing—but to practice with the heart, mind, and body; with commitment, vow, and dedication; with great faith, great doubt, and great determination—then you have the manifested Sangha Treasure. Everything else is a cheap imitation. It just looks like the real thing.

Finally we come to the abiding Three Treasures. Converting gods and liberating people, appearing in vast space or in a speck of dust, is the Buddha Treasure of the abiding Three Treasures. To abide means to preserve and protect. We need to appreciate that our practice is not only about our own realization, about relieving our own pain and suffering; it is also about relieving the pain and suffering of all beings. We should never lose sight of that. We remind ourselves every night of that fact at the monastery by reciting the bodhisattva vows.

We are the vessel of the dharma at this time and this place. What we do each sitting, each moment, with our work, with our zazen and services, with our vows, not only affirms and verifies the enlightenment of the Buddha and all the past Buddhas but also preserves and protects the dharma so it will be available for future generations.

We are part of the transmission of the dharma from East to West. It goes from place to place only through people. Only a Buddha can realize Buddha. Only a Buddha can practice Buddhadharma. Only a Buddha is a vessel of the dharma. All sentient beings are Buddhas. All Buddhas are sentient beings. What we do, therefore, is no small thing. Our actions have far-reaching consequences. The karma of taking refuge, of making the vow to save all sentient beings, vowing to realize oneself, to practice zazen, to nurture the mountains and rivers, to work in the garden—all of it is part of the legacy that has come down to us for twenty-six hundred years and, it is hoped, will continue twenty-six hundred years into the future. If it does, it is because of how we take care of it.

We include in the abiding Buddha Treasure those Buddhas made of wood, metal, stone, and paint. All of them are manifestations of the infinite boundless Buddhas present in the myriad realms. Each of these Buddhas is presently expounding the dharma, converting and saving all beings, healing and nourishing all beings, according to the karma of circumstances. Do we really understand the truth of that statement? The wooden Buddha on the altar is expounding the dharma according to karma. How do we understand that? Common sense is not going to help us here. Scientific knowledge is not going to help us. There is another realm of human experience involved.

What does it mean to bow to the Buddha, specifically to that wooden Buddha on the altar? A monk asked Zen Master Chao-chou, "What is Buddha?" Chao-chou said, "He's on the altar." What did Chao-chou mean? How is that piece of wood a Buddha? Is that painting a Buddha? Do not separate yourself from anything! Do not separate yourself from the chanting, from your vow, from your commitment, from each other, from this whole great earth.

Transformed into the sutras and converted into the oceanic storehouse, the Dharma of the abiding Three Treasures delivers the inanimate and animate, saving all beings. What are the sutras? The spirit of these precepts, the spirit of the sutras, the spirit of this discourse, goes far beyond the words. We cannot reach them with our analytical minds alone. This teaching is dark to the mind; we have to sense it with our heart, our feelings.

The Sangha of the abiding Three Treasures is saving all beings from all suffering, releasing them from the abode of the three realms—the realms of desire, form, and formlessness. In order to save all beings from suffering, we need to put an end to the three poisons of greed, anger, and ignorance.

Having appreciated the Three Treasures from the three different perspectives, we need to appreciate the unity or the oneness of these three perspectives. Each interpenetrates the other. The Buddha, the Dharma, and the Sangha completely merge and are one reality. What is that reality? This dharma is incredibly profound and infinitely subtle. Because of its profundity and subtlety, it requires whole body and mind engagement for it to communicate.

Taking refuge is not a matter of casual encounter. This is a whole body-and-mind vow, whole body-and-mind unity, whole body-and-mind commitment. Those who give that much, realize it. Those who do not, do not realize it. Some may realize it, some may not. Either way is okay. It is up to us. Nobody can do it for us. Buddha could not do it for us, if he were here. Only we have the power to take advantage of the personal karma that has placed us in this time and place. It is a unique opportunity, and how we use it is totally in our hands.

In order to reach our full human potential, we must live completely and die completely. In order for this practice to function, it needs to be engaged. It does not happen automatically because we put on a robe, attend a retreat, or read a book on Zen—"Okay, I'm here. Now do me, Dharma." It does not happen that way. We have to work for it. We have to put ourselves on the line. We have to practice the edge of our life in order to receive the dharma. Undeniably, it is here. We are surrounded, interpenetrated, enveloped, and swallowed by it. But most of us are blind and deaf to it. We do not see it. We do not hear it. We do not feel it. When will we wake up?

The First Pure Precept

NOT CREATING EVIL

On the surface, the Three Pure Precepts—"not creating evil," "practicing good," and "actualizing good for others"—seem rather simplistic. In reality, they are a bottomless source of teachings, critically relevant in our day-to-day practice of Zen, and in our lives.

The precepts begin where the intimacy that encompasses heaven and earth is realized. "Not creating evil" is the fundamental teaching of Buddhism. It is the central pillar of our practice. The Three Pure Precepts are pure because they are absolute. They are pure because they reach everywhere. Evil has no independent existence. It is dependent upon its creator. The same can be said for the entire phenomenal universe, and for each one of us. We are all interdependent entities.

When you look at the Ten Grave Precepts from the perspective of the Three Pure Precepts, "not creating evil" is do not kill, do not steal, do not misuse sexuality, do not lie, do not cloud the mind, do not speak of others' errors and faults, do not elevate the self and blame others, do not be withholding, do not be angry, and do not defile the Three Treasures. "Practicing good" is the other side of "not creating evil." "Practicing good" is affirm life, be giving, honor the body, manifest truth, proceed clearly, see the perfection, realize self and other as one, give generously, actualize harmony, and experience the intimacy of things.

Each of the Ten Grave Precepts expresses how not to create evil and how to practice good. One side is affirmative; one side is prohibitive. They work together. They are interdependent and arise mutually. "Actualizing good for others" is nothing other than the mutual identity of "not creating evil" and "practicing good." It is the great heart of Kannon Bodhisattva manifesting in the world as compassion.

Good and evil are very difficult to define because moral values are relative. They are relative to culture, personal preference, and social customs; to time, place, position, and degree. Because it is difficult to nail this down, we return to the fundamental understanding of the Three Pure Precepts. Good is understood differently in different worlds and different times. Still, the human mind is originally neither good nor evil. Good and evil always arise in accord with circumstances. They are created. "Not creating" is therefore quintessential.

The unique contribution of the Buddhist precepts in the domain of religious morality is that they go beyond moral excellence. What they address is how to protect morality from legalism, conformity, and moralism. While maintaining authenticity and freedom, we do not retreat from moral involvement. It is because people do not fully understand what is meant by "the human mind is originally beyond good and evil" that we entertain the deluded view that Zen is somehow amoral. Unequivocally, Zen is not beyond morality. Zen functions in the world of good and evil. At the same time, it is not hindered by good and evil. That is the moral freedom of these incredible teachings.

Essentially, the nature of morality is empty. To realize that does not, however, lead to nihilism or anarchy. Realization does not entail an "anything goes" attitude. The pivotal focus of practice with the precepts is how to live in the world of relativity, without falling into the trap of being distracted and disturbed by the ten thousand things. How do we realize absolute freedom and purity in the midst of a world fragmented by good and evil?

Since good and evil have no metaphysical ground or independent self-nature, how do they spring into being? How does evil appear? By creating. That is why not creating any evil is intrinsic to realization, intrinsic to enlightenment. In other words, to commit evil is incompatible with enlightenment. Enlightenment without morality is not authentic enlightenment. From a Buddhist point of view, morality can never be fully authenticated without enlightenment. Morality and enlightenment are thoroughly interdependent.

Enlightened or deluded, we all live within the intricate maze of the laws of cause and effect. It is an inescapable fact that morality functions in the world of duality. The precepts exist to deal with that infinite range of phenomena. They are based on absolute nature and emerge out of the realization of no-self. But no-self does not function. The functioning of the wisdom of absolute nature manifests as the precepts, as compassion.

Evil is neither nonexistent nor existent; there is simply "not creating." Evil is neither empty nor formed; there is simply "not creating." Evil is not moral, amoral, or moralistic but simply "not creating." In Buddhism, there is no "thou shall not" coming down to us from on high. "I will not," reflecting a kind of self-centered autonomy, does not apply either. What the precepts are about is noncontrivance. Morality, if it is going to be authentic, can and must arise spontaneously from enlightenment. Morality and enlightenment are not to be understood in terms of cause and effect, or means and end.

When morality becomes effortless, purposeless, and playful, it becomes the nonmoral morality of the Buddhas and ancestors. That is the culmination of formal Zen training. At that time, morality, art, and play merge together as one thing. One teacher said, "When 'ought' becomes 'is' in the transparency of thusness, only then do we come to the highest morality."

How do you not create evil? We must first understand the relationship between evil and its creation. Mutual arising and identity characterize the nature of reality. Every aspect and juncture contains the totality. That is the way it is with thought and reality. That is the way it is with the senses—the eye, the form that the eye sees, and consciousness together create what we call reality. They are interdependent—one cannot exist without the other.

The ten thousand things do not obstruct each other. Interpenetration and interdependence exist mutually, without hindrance. They do not get in each other's way. Water does not hinder water. The whole universe and its myriad forms are all used without hindrance.

When we hold on to the precepts, we are trapped in the cage of the precepts. If you get caught up in the hierarchies or the grid of rules, if there is any trace of concept or contrivance, you are like a demon haunting the fields, trapped in a self-created labyrinth. With the slightest choice of good and evil your mind falls into confusion. If these precepts are used as rules, they lose a lot of their value. We get stuck in them. When Kannon Bodhisattva with her ten thousand hands is responding to the cries of the world, there is no contrivance, no concept, no knowing. She has no idea of what she is doing—she is blind, deaf, and dumb. That in itself is not creating evil.

If we are not aware of the precepts, of their existence, of how Buddhas live their lives in the world of differences and suffering, then it is very easy to go on our way, merrily creating all sorts of karma. But once

we are aware of the precepts and see that there does exist a way of understanding how we fit into this vast universe, how we can function in a way that is nourishing and healing and in harmony with things, we create a cutting edge to work with. That cutting edge is a challenge to each one of us. It is one thing to cast off body and mind, it is quite another thing to have realized "cast-off body and mind" and to manifest that realization in the world. At that point our way of perceiving ourselves and the universe, of combusting our lives among the ten thousand things, is completely transformed.

The Second Pure
Precept

_____

PRACTICING GOOD

Zen Master Dogen said: *Practice all that is good. All that is good is the good of the three natures—good, bad, and neutral. Although good exists within the nature of good, it does not mean that good has some previous, independent existence and is waiting to be accomplished. When good is done, it contains all good. Although good is formless, when it is done, it attracts more good faster than a magnet attracts iron. Its power is stronger than the strongest wind. All the accumulated karma throughout the earth, mountains, rivers, world, and lands cannot obstruct the power of good.*

The Three Pure Precepts are an open-ended and very profound teaching. In the world, they manifest as the Ten Grave Precepts. When the ground out of which the Three Pure Precepts emerge hasn't been fully appreciated, there is always the danger that the Ten Grave Precepts will degenerate into a mere collection of rules. That is not what the precepts are. The precepts are a way of life that has to be intimately experienced, digested, and actualized. As we work with the Second Pure Precept, "practice good," we should keep in mind the power of what we're dealing with and attend it with great care.

We say that the precepts are the definition of the life of a Buddha; they describe how an enlightened being lives in the world. Early in their practice students have not had that premise confirmed by their experience. They have the word of the teacher, the ancestors, and the sutras to go by, but they do not know it personally. And it is personal experience that is the bottom line in this practice, not understanding or belief. Zen is a practice that requires one to empower oneself, to realize for oneself everything that the Buddhas and ancestors have realized for themselves. That in itself is the mind-to-mind transmission.

As practice evolves, the precepts, originally accepted as an act of faith, become the very fabric of our life. This transformation occurs if the practice is conducted properly. The practice of the precepts takes time. It continuously deepens and broadens. In the beginning they are a collection of rules: do not kill, do not steal, do not elevate the self and put down others. Shut the door, turn out the light, wash the dishes. With time we realize what the Three Pure Precepts really entail. We realize what the practice of the Ten Grave Precepts really means. We realize atonement. Then this matter of ongoing practice becomes very personal and immediate. Ultimately, the precepts interfuse with our life. People who have come to the "end" of their practice without the precepts as part of their lives probably do so because the precepts were never a part of their practice all along the way.

When we transcend all attachments, concepts, and views, the true dharma eye is opened, the exquisite teaching of formless form is manifested. Actualized in the world of good and evil, it is not of good and evil. It is the endless spring of peaceful dwelling, reaching everywhere. The state of clarity described by these words is attained when we free ourselves of the entanglements of dualities, ridding ourselves of views, concepts, and attachments. It is not something acquired as a result of practice. It is something revealed as a result of practice. Once you come to realization, the teaching of formless form and the true dharma eye begin to actualize in the world of good and evil. This realization arises from a place where there is no good and no evil, no heaven and no earth; no eye, ear, nose, tongue, body, mind; no enlightenment, no delusion, no nirvana. Yet it manifests in a world where there is good and evil, heaven and hell, cause and effect. At the same time, it is not, in and of itself, good or evil.

Good neither exists nor does not exist. It is simply practice. It is manifested through practice. "Practicing good" is practice itself. Good is not form; it is not emptiness; it is just practice. "Practicing good" falls into neither of those extremes. It is neither being nor nonbeing, neither existence nor nonexistence, neither form nor emptiness; it is just practice.

"Practicing good" is not a moral injunction but rather realization itself. It is not a contrivance. The moment the mind moves, it is no longer "practicing good." The witness that is always watching needs to dissolve, just like it does in zazen. If, in your zazen, you are following the breath and you are watching yourself follow the breath, that scrutiny separates you from the breath. There can be no "falling away of body and mind." The witness, in noticing, is saying, "I exist." It constantly reaffirms the illusion that there is a self. The skin bag gets thicker and thicker.

Morality, in order to be authentic, needs to arise out of one's own realization. It is because the self is empty that "not creating evil," "practicing good," and "actualizing good for others" make any sense at all. When morality spontaneously springs forth from one's own attainment, it is effortless, purposeless, and even playful. It is a delightful morality.

The Sixteen Precepts of the Buddha Way are the most profound teaching of morality that I have ever seen. They are alive, vital, and responsive to circumstances. Good and evil are always conditioned and dependent upon circumstances. The whole phenomenal universe is nothing but conditioned existence. Every speck of dust is dependent upon everything else in the universe. You cannot affect one thing without affecting the totality.

We should understand, too, that good is not an object. It is not an entity or a condition that the practitioner deals with. It is just practicing. It does not exist independently but arises in accord with the circumstances, in the specific context of a particular time, place, position, and degree of action. A single event, seen from two different perspectives, can appear good from one angle and bad from another. Someone pointing a gun at me pulls the trigger: bad karma. He fires, I duck: good karma. The bullet hits the person standing behind me: bad karma. Same bullet, three scenarios. Good and evil always appear and operate within a reference system. They need to be seen in terms of that reference system in order for the action to be evaluated.

Time, place, position, and degree need to be considered in appreciating any action.

The historical period of time is tightly interwoven with the generally accepted notion of morality. There are scenes on television these days that were outrageous and censored twenty-five years ago. Language I used as a boatswain's mate in the navy in 1947, and was chewed out for by the officers, is common on prime-time programs today. What was inappropriate in the past is acceptable now.

Place also affects how an action appears. Wearing my priestly robes addressing an assembly of students is perfectly appropriate. Wearing my robes at the downtown diner is questionable. There is nothing wrong with the robes; it is the place that makes the difference.

The position or role we play in a relationship also makes all the difference in the world in how we function. What we do as a parent, what we do as a lover, and what we do as a teacher may differ dramatically. The act may be the same, but in those various roles the moral quality of the act shifts.

The degree of action, its intensity, is another parameter affecting the moral nature of an act. It needs to be just the right amount. It needs to match the encountered conditions. Sometimes a whisper is just as powerful and penetrating as a thunderous roar. Time, place, position, and degree form the matrix within which the precepts function.

Good and evil, self and others, absolute and relative, being and nonbeing, are all interrelated and interpenetrated entities. Good and evil occur in the world. Yet, even if evil envelops the entire earth and the whole universe, there is still "not creating evil" and "practicing good." "Not creating evil" and "practicing good" are not hindered at all by the omnipresence of evil. That is the depth and extent of the Pure Precepts and realization.

Master Dogen said: *Since time immemorial, Buddhas and ancestors have continuously taught, "Practice good." Although good is practice and practice is good, it is not the self that does good, and it is not known to the self. Further, it is not other, nor is it known to the other. Practice is not being or nonbeing, not form or emptiness: it is just practice. In practice, all that is good is realized and actualized.*

In "practicing good" it is not the self that does good. The self is forgotten. "To forget the self is to be enlightened by the ten thousand things. To be enlightened by the ten thousand things is to cast away one's body and mind and the body and mind of others." That is the source of the Pure Precepts.

The presence of self, the subtlest hint of self-centeredness, creates the difference between a "do-gooder" and the manifestation of true compassion. In compassion, in practicing good, there is no agent that is doing good and no one who benefits from it; there is no subject or object. There is not even any sense of doing. Compassion happens. It happens the way you grow your hair. There is no effort involved. It is not the self that does good; "the doing of good" is not even known to the self. Knowing depends on the words and ideas that describe reality. There is no intimacy in knowing. Knowing involves the knower and the thing that the knower knows, and that implies separation. This practice has nothing to do with knowledge. It is the experience of intimacy.

Doing good in complete intimacy is the embodiment and activity of the ten thousand hands and eyes of Kannon Bodhisattva, the bodhisattva of compassion. She is called "the hearer of the cries of the world." She is the bodhisattva who responds when someone cries out for help. When she responds, she responds in perfect accord with circumstances. She doesn't always appear in the form of a goddess, or even necessarily in a female form. She may appear in male form, or in nonhuman form. She may appear as a god or devil. She responds without mind. There is no thought. Kannon does not know about goodness. She doesn't know about doing. Compassion arises spontaneously out of wisdom: the realization of no separation. Someone falls; you pick the person up. There is no effort.

People wonder about such an esoteric teaching. Where is this goddess? Why don't we see her? Every time a car breaks down on the highway or a lonely road and a motorist stops to give aid, that's Kannon Bodhisattva manifesting in the form of a motorist coming to the aid of another. If she's going to help a drunk in a bar, she'll probably appear as another drunk, not as a holy being glowing with light.

It's kind of interesting how this happens. A couple of weeks ago I was watching a news report about two Weimaraner dogs, 175 pounds each. The two of them broke loose and attacked a ten-year-old girl. The girl started screaming for help. Bursting out of a nearby house came a little old woman. The broadcast had her on camera. She was cut up and scarred, and she couldn't have weighed more than a hundred pounds. She was short, almost like a bird. She had laid into those dogs and started punching them, hitting them, pulling them, and throwing herself on top of the child. Finally she dragged the child into a swampy pond—it wasn't water, just a bunch of muck and mud. Somehow the muck and mud confused the dogs and broke them from their killer trance and they ran off.

The reporter said to the woman: "You're a hero." And the woman seemed stunned by that. She was looking at the reporter quizzically. She said, "But the little girl cried out, 'Please help me! They're going to kill me.' Over and over again. How could I not go?" There was no sense of self in this woman's action. The girl wasn't her daughter. This woman was totally vulnerable, yet totally invulnerable because of no-self. This is the ten thousand hands and eyes of Kannon Bodhisattva. This is the intimacy of doing good with no attachment to self.

It's very easy to understand not attaching to things that are evil or dualistic. But the same problem exists when we attach to good, to Buddhism, to the absolute. We need to realize that practice is not being or nonbeing, not form or emptiness: it is just practice. "Just practice" is suchness. It is this very moment, transcending all dualities. "Just practice" contains no past and no future. It is always right here, right now.

So, why should it be so difficult? In a way, it is, and in a way, it is not. In ancient China, the Pang family took up this point during one of their famous dharma dialogues. Layman Pang, Laywoman Pang, and their daughter, all enlightened practitioners, were sitting around their living room. Layman Pang said, "Difficult, difficult, difficult—like trying to find a needle in the haystack." Laywoman Pang followed, "Easy, easy, easy—like your feet touching the ground when you step out of bed." And the daughter concluded, "Neither difficult nor easy—the teachings of the dharma on the tips of the ten thousand grasses."

It all depends on what, and how much, we need to work with and work through. We can call it our karma. Whatever it is we consistently hold on to continually re-creates the illusion of a self. You cannot forget the self until you have put to rest all of the self-centered convolutions, subtle or overt, holy or profane. The person who is dealing with a holy past, walking around with palms in gassho, halo around the head, may have just as much difficulty in practice as a person affected by a profane past. Sacredness, too, can be a sticking place. It does not matter whether you cling to a BMW or the dharma; they both separate you from the truth. In a sense, there is no distinction between holy and unholy. Both create karma that needs to be transcended before we can realize ourselves. That is why true realization is so rare.

So, "practice good." Go by yourself and you will meet it everywhere. It is just you yourself. And yet, you are not it. If you see it in this way, you can be as you are and always have been—perfect, complete, lacking nothing. That is the life of all Buddhas. That is the life of all sentient beings—my life and your life. When we realize that truth, we make the Buddha's life our own.

The Third Pure Precept

ACTUALIZING GOOD FOR OTHERS

Without the moral and ethical teachings there is no true Buddhadharma. Without Buddhadharma, there are no true moral and ethical teachings. Enlightenment and morality are one reality. This statement has perturbed people over the ages and given rise to misunderstandings and concerns that until we are enlightened, we remain immoral. We need to understand that Zen Master Dogen's statement "There is no enlightenment without morality and no morality without enlightenment" arises directly from his equation "Practice is enlightenment." All sentient beings are already perfect and complete, already enlightened, but for most people that enlightenment has not yet been realized. When we practice, we manifest that enlightenment. Practice is not a means to attain enlightenment but the manifestation of enlightenment itself. When we practice the precepts, we manifest that same enlightenment. The precepts are the definition of the life of a Buddha.

The Three Pure Precepts are "pure" by virtue of their all-encompassing nature. We sometimes refer to them as the unadulterated precepts because they are without defilement. The reason they are without defilement is that they include everything. There is nothing outside of them to stain them. They are absolute. They fill the whole universe. Indeed, they are the whole universe itself.

The basis of the precepts is the absolute basis of reality, the realization of no-self. But no-self does not function in the world, amid the daily turmoil and distractions. How do we make it function? It manifests in a form that is in accord with the circumstances; at the same time, it is not hindered by those same circumstances. Manifested in the world, "actualizing good for others" becomes the life of a bodhisattva.

The first pure precept, "not creating evil," pertains to the negative side of the Grave Precepts, the prohibitions and restrictions. The second pure precept, "practicing good," is the positive side. It invites and affirms our involvement. For the Ten Grave Precepts to be functioning smoothly, both sides need to be studied and implemented. When both aspects of the Pure Precepts are working fluidly, we have "actualizing good for others." "Actualizing good for others" functions with the realization that there is no self or other. It is because there is no self and other that there is "actualizing good for others." "Actualizing good for others" is the life of a bodhisattva.

Dogen spoke of four ways that a bodhisattva acts to benefit all beings, four means of leading sentient beings to freedom. The bodhisattvas use these methods to enable people to do good, to avoid evil, and to follow the Way. The first is "giving," both spiritual and material. The second is "loving words" or "loving speech." The third is "benefiting humans by good conduct of body, speech, and mind." Another way to express that is "service for the welfare of all beings." The fourth is "identity with others," assuming the same form as that of the sentient beings to be benefited, "appearing in vast space or in a speck of dust." The poor help the poor; the homeless help the homeless; the depraved help the depraved; the gods help the gods.

What Dogen emphasized in his teachings on "giving" is the way and the spirit in which the giving takes place. True giving means that the giver and the receiver are one reality. When giving happens that way, it is not about doing good anymore. Often, in order to do good, we subtly need to be better than the person we are helping. We reach down into the decay and help the downtrodden, the less fortunate, the helpless. That is not the practice of a bodhisattva. The bodhisattva does not practice from a distance. He or she is right there with those being assisted, covered with the same mud. They climb out together, because self and other are not two separate entities. The giving of a bodhisattva is effortless and purposeless. There is no payoff, no hidden gold.

The principle of "no payoff" applies to everything we do. Routinely, when we wash the dishes, we do it to have clean dishes. That is the payoff—nice, clean dishes to eat from. We rake the lawn in order to have a clean lawn. We tune up a car to have an engine that is running efficiently. That is one way of doing our tasks—very goal oriented. But there is also another hibitions and restrictions. The second pure precept, "practicing good," is the positive side. It invites and affirms our involvement. For the Ten Grave Precepts to be functioning smoothly, both sides need to be studied and implemented. When both aspects of the Pure Precepts are working fluidly, we have "actualizing good for others." "Actualizing good for others" functions with the realization that there is no self or other. It is because there is no self and other that there is "actualizing good for others." "Actualizing good for others" is the life of a bodhisattva.

Dogen spoke of four ways that a bodhisattva acts to benefit all beings, four means of leading sentient beings to freedom. The bodhisattvas use these methods to enable people to do good, to avoid evil, and to follow the Way. The first is "giving," both spiritual and material. The second is "loving words" or "loving speech." The third is "benefiting humans by good conduct of body, speech, and mind." Another way to express that is "service for the welfare of all beings." The fourth is "identity with others," assuming the same form as that of the sentient beings to be benefited, "appearing in vast space or in a speck of dust." The poor help the poor; the homeless help the homeless; the depraved help the depraved; the gods help the gods.

What Dogen emphasized in his teachings on "giving" is the way and the spirit in which the giving takes place. True giving means that the giver and the receiver are one reality. When giving happens that way, it is not about doing good anymore. Often, in order to do good, we subtly need to be better than the person we are helping. We reach down into the decay and help the downtrodden, the less fortunate, the helpless. That is not the practice of a bodhisattva. The bodhisattva does not practice from a distance. He or she is right there with those being assisted, covered with the same mud. They climb out together, because self and other are not two separate entities. The giving of a bodhisattva is effortless and purposeless. There is no payoff, no hidden gold.

The principle of "no payoff" applies to everything we do. Routinely, when we wash the dishes, we do it to have clean dishes. That is the payoff—nice, clean dishes to eat from. We rake the lawn in order to have a clean lawn. We tune up a car to have an engine that is running efficiently. That is one way of doing our tasks—very goal oriented. But there is also another way of doing it. We can wash the dishes simply to wash the dishes; not to have clean dishes, but only and completely to wash them. We can rake the lawn, not to have a clean lawn, but just to rake the lawn. We can tune up a car to tune up a car. We actualize good for all beings, not to be a wonderful person and gain nirvana points, but just to actualize good. To actualize good for others is not to create evil and to practice good.

About the second way the bodhisattva helps others, Dogen said:

Loving speech means that as you meet sentient beings, you first arouse the sense of compassion in your mind and treat them with considerate, affectionate words. It is altogether devoid of any violent and spiteful language. Thoughtful words arise from the mind of loving-kindness, and the mind of loving-kindness has compassion as its seed. Loving speech has the power to influence even an emperor's mind. It is not just to speak only highly of others' strengths and achievements.

In a sense, "loving speech" is easy to use and misuse. Every slick politician and salesman is trained in manipulating words, sometimes sweet words. But where is the speech coming from? What is the intent?

Is there anything to be gained? If there is even one iota of ego in it, the speech becomes self-serving. It is only when speech arises from no-self that it can truly be called loving speech. Then it nourishes and heals.

"Benefiting humans by good conduct of body, speech, and mind" or "working for the welfare of all beings" means that we create ways to benefit all sentient beings, whoever they might be or whatever their status. Dogen said:

Commiserate with a turtle in trouble. Take care of the sparrow suffering from injury. When you see the distressed turtle or watch the sick sparrow, you do not expect any repayment for your favor, but you are moved entirely by your desire to help others. Then he added, Therefore, serve enemies and friends equally, and assist self and other without discrimination. If you grasp this truth, you will see that this is the reason that even the grass and trees, the wind and water, are all naturally engaged in the activity of profiting others, and your understanding will certainly serve the other's benefit.

These guidelines are not a collection of simplistic rules to be followed blindly. They need to be turned inside out and understood experientially. Sometimes, way of doing it. We can wash the dishes simply to wash the dishes; not to have clean dishes, but only and completely to wash them. We can rake the lawn, not to have a clean lawn, but just to rake the lawn. We can tune up a car to tune up a car. We actualize good for all beings, not to be a wonderful person and gain nirvana points, but just to actualize good. To actualize good for others is not to create evil and to practice good.

About the second way the bodhisattva helps others, Dogen said:

Loving speech means that as you meet sentient beings, you first arouse the sense of compassion in your mind and treat them with considerate, affectionate words. It is altogether devoid of any violent and spiteful language. Thoughtful words arise from the mind of loving-kindness, and the mind of loving-kindness has compassion as its seed. Loving speech has the power to influence even an emperor's mind. It is not just to speak only highly of others' strengths and achievements.

In a sense, "loving speech" is easy to use and misuse. Every slick politician and salesman is trained in manipulating words, sometimes sweet words. But where is the speech coming from? What is the intent?

Is there anything to be gained? If there is even one iota of ego in it, the speech becomes self-serving. It is only when speech arises from no-self that it can truly be called loving speech. Then it nourishes and heals.

"Benefiting humans by good conduct of body, speech, and mind" or "working for the welfare of all beings" means that we create ways to benefit all sentient beings, whoever they might be or whatever their status. Dogen said:

Commiserate with a turtle in trouble. Take care of the sparrow suffering from injury. When you see the distressed turtle or watch the sick sparrow, you do not expect any repayment for your favor, but you are moved entirely by your desire to help others. Then he added, Therefore, serve enemies and friends equally, and assist self and other without discrimination. If you grasp this truth, you will see that this is the reason that even the grass and trees, the wind and water, are all naturally engaged in the activity of profiting others, and your understanding will certainly serve the other's benefit.

These guidelines are not a collection of simplistic rules to be followed blindly. They need to be turned inside out and understood experientially. Sometimes, in taking away, there is giving. A master said, "If you have a staff, I'll give you one. If you don't have a staff, I'll take it away." We need to understand giving from that perspective. Loving speech may on the surface sound harsh—for instance, the monitor in the zendo yelling, "Wake up!" But that shout is not self-serving; it is compassionate. If anger is really expressed for the benefit of others, it is loving anger. The mother who scolds her child playing out on the street is using loving words if she is yelling for the benefit and well-being of that child. A car salesman's obsequious manner perverts loving speech when the flatteries are dispatched to get another model off the showroom floor. Walking around with a smile, patting everybody on the back, saying "Have a good day" is not the way of a bodhisattva.

Finally, there is "identity with others." Identity with others is nondifference. It applies equally to the self and to others. What you do to others you do to yourself. How you treat yourself is how you treat others. Self and other are one indivisible thusness, the mutual identity of all things. To realize this is to free oneself of birth and death.

"Giving," "loving speech," "working for the welfare of others," and "assuming the same form as that

of various sentient beings to be benefited" are the virtues of Kannon Bodhisattva. Every time a person is
suffering in pain and someone comes along to allevi-
ate that suffering, that is a manifestation of Kannon
Bodhisattva. The physician aiding someone who is injured; the homeless man helping a drunk who has
fallen down and hit his head—these instances are
nothing other than the virtue of Kannon Bodhisattva
manifested in a particular form. It is the life of each
one of us.

We should appreciate that our coming and going
always take place right here, right now. "No coming,
no going" includes birth and death. In birth, not a
particle is added; in death, not an atom is lost. In ar-
riving, there is no gain; in departing, there is no loss.
The Diamond Net of Indra reaches everywhere—
past, present, and future. Nothing is excluded. That
is why we can say, "No self, no other, nothing to
choose, nothing to discard." Where would it go?
Where would it come from? "Endless blue mountains
without a speck of dust" refers to these very mountains and rivers themselves, each one undefiled, perfect and complete, containing everything.

"Not creating evil," "practicing good," and "actualizing good for others" are the Three Pure Precepts
upon which all of the moral teachings of the Buddha

are based. All of the precepts arise out of them. And what are they? The life of each one of us. We should realize there is no place to put this gigantic body. It reaches everywhere.

The Ten Grave Precepts

Wisdom Mind

The precepts contain the totality of the teachings of the Buddhadharma. This is not immediately apparent, and it may take us ten to twenty years of practice before we really see it and actualize it in our lives. But it is all there. Totally engaged and thoroughly appreciated, the precepts continue to be a bottomless source of wisdom, helping us to embrace our full human potential, our Buddha nature. These precepts are the most complete and far-reaching facet of the dharma I could possibly share.

People inquire about practice. "What is lay practice?" *Kai*—the precepts. "What is monastic practice?" Kai—the precepts. "What is home practice?" Kai—the precepts. "What is the sacred?"—Kai. "What is the secular?"—Kai. Everything we see, everything we touch, everything we do, our way of relating, is right here in these precepts. They are the Buddha Way, the heart of the Buddha. The full spectrum of emotions, the love, the compassion, the all-embracing mind of clear wisdom, filling the whole universe—it is all here in these sixteen precepts.

The Three Pure Precepts—"not creating evil," "practicing good," and "actualizing good for others" —define the natural order of reality. If you eschew evil, practice good, and actualize good for others, you are in harmony with the myriad dharmas that make up this universe. Not creating evil is "the abiding place of all Buddhas." Practicing good is "the dharma of samyak-sambodhi, the way of all beings." Actualizing good for others is "to transcend the profane and go beyond the holy, to liberate oneself and others." Obviously, it is straightforward to acknowledge the Three Pure Precepts, but how do we make them function in our lives? How can we practice them? How do we not create evil? How do we practice good? How do we actualize good for others?

The way to do that is shown in the Ten Grave Precepts, which reveal the precise activity of the Three

Pure Precepts. Traditionally, the Grave Precepts were expressed as prohibitions. In our training we have included an affirmative expression of the precepts as well. They state both what not to do and what to do. Consequently, they balance passivity with activity, dismantling our tendencies to withdraw from the challenges, the complexities, and the turmoil of modern living.

First Grave Precept
Affirm life. Do not kill.

Taking the life of any living being is a violation of the first grave precept. Yet there is a continuous killing that is taking place. We all take part in it. We kill to sustain our life. The hierarchy of life that is commonly accepted among humans, with us on top of the ladder and cows and cabbages below, is an arbitrary one. Life is life. It is all sacred—the tiniest insect, a carrot, a chicken, a human being. All the food we take is life. That is the way it is on Earth. There are no creatures on the face of this planet that take a meal without doing so at the expense of another life.

To consume life is a characteristic of our biological existence. Because of the intimate appreciation of that fact, the occasion of mindfully receiving food in a formal monastery meal is a profound ritual in our tradition. Its purpose is not to take lightly that which we are receiving. To eat is to receive the sacrament of life. We consume life to sustain our life, and to affirm all life. There is no question that human life should be valued very highly, but at the same time, the life of all beings should be respected and treasured. We tend to snatch away the lives of other creatures too readily, disturbing the balance in the environment whenever it suits us.

Self-centeredness is one sure way to violate any precept. If an act is completed solely for the benefit of oneself, that in itself is a violation. It is deluded. There is no self. It is self-centeredness that creates a uniquely human kind of conflict and violence, violence that is not seen among any other species. What we have done to each other throughout history and what we continue to do to each other is sad, appalling, and terribly deluded. This kind of violence is definitely not in harmony with the self-evident laws of the universe. It continually disturbs the growth and development of the ten thousand things in nature, and it destroys the seed of compassion and the reverence for life that emanate from the Buddha nature.

Clearly, it is not possible for humans to live without killing. Our immune systems are constantly fending off invading microbes. If our white cells did not kill we would not survive a day. But the spirit of the first grave precept, from the literal point of view, is to exert oneself totally in observing the precept to the best of one's ability.

From the perspective of compassion and reverence for life, we should be clear that this precept means to refrain from killing the mind of compassion and reverence. Also, and this is a very subtle point, an aspect of observing this precept includes killing with the sword of compassion when necessary. Several years ago I was driving along the highway and a raccoon walked out under the wheels of my car. I ran over it. Looking in the rearview mirror, I could see it on the road, still moving. I stopped the car and went back. It was pretty young, badly crushed, and crying out in terrible pain. My own self-centeredness, squeamishness, and fear prevented me from taking its life and putting it out of its misery. I could have just driven the car back over it. But I could not bring myself to do that. I left it on the highway and drove away. In so doing, I killed the mind of compassion and reverence for life that was inside me. I violated the precept "do not kill," because I did not have the heart to kill that raccoon. My own feelings were more important than the agony of that creature.

If you have not yet seen into Buddha nature, it is very difficult to understand the precepts from the perspective of Buddha nature. This is their central pillar and why it is vital to practice them through faith until there is a full awakening, a direct firsthand appreciation that they are the complete expression of the life of a Buddha.

Buddha nature never dies. The realm of Buddha nature is completely beyond dualism. As a result, you cannot oppose killing and nonkilling against each other. There is no killing, there is no being killed, and there is no one to kill. To give rise to the thought "to kill" instantly violates the precepts from this perspective. The thought itself is essentially deluded.

Zen Master Bodhidharma commented on each of the Ten Grave Precepts. He called them the One-Mind Precepts. In talking about the first precept, he said, "Self-nature is inconceivably wondrous. In the everlasting dharma, not giving rise to the notion of extinction is called the precept of refraining from taking life." Master Dogen said, "In affirming life and refraining from taking life, you allow the Buddha seed to grow, and thereby inherit the Buddha's wisdom. Do not destroy life. Life is not killing. Do not kill life."

There is no hierarchy in understanding the precepts in these three ways. Their appreciation is not progressive. In hearing about multiple ways of understanding, there is an immediate tendency to stratify the teachings, claiming that one way of seeing is more advanced and complete than another. We may think that to understand the precepts literally is inferior to understanding them from the one-mind point of view. That is not the case. The precepts and their various applications are totally interpenetrated, interdependent, having a mutual causality. One does not exist without the other. They create a matrix, a moral and karmic matrix.

There is a proper spirit of working with the precepts. We should appreciate that spirit. We can approach them with an intention to absorb them into our being, or we can see them as obstructions that need to be avoided or negotiated. In seeing them as barriers to our freedom we end up looking for loopholes. We bump up against the precepts and rationalize and justify our actions.

The loopholes will go on forever. The Buddha tried to close some of them during his lifetime. His effort resulted in the lengthy list of rules contained in the Vinaya. When the rule of celibacy was introduced, monastics said, "Celibacy only applies to a man-woman relationship. So, a man-man relationship is permitted." Homosexuality flourished. Rules had to be adapted. One monastic had a sexual relationship with a monkey, another with a dead body. Animals had to be included in the celibacy rule, and corpses. And on and on and on. The rules grew in number as the creativity in breaking them grew.

The attitude of trying to outsmart the precepts reminds me of the way my six-year-old son would react to my disciplinary measures. I remember sitting at the dinner table with my two arguing sons. Fed up with all the noise, I shouted, "Johnny, shut your mouth and eat!" He closed his mouth and poured the food against his tightly shut lips so it ran down his chest. In comprehending the spirit of the precepts, and their relationship to our Buddha nature, there is no need for all the extra regulations and injunctions. There is simply the freedom of living our life wisely and harmoniously.

Second Grave Precept

Be giving. Do not steal.

The verse from Bodhidharma's One-Mind Precept says, "Self-nature is inconceivably wondrous. In the dharma in which nothing can be obtained, not giving rise to the thought of obtaining is called the precept of refraining from stealing." All of the One-Mind Pre-

cepts of Bodhidharma start with the statement, "Self-nature is inconceivably wondrous." That is a direct expression of realization. It is the Buddha nature's expression of Buddha nature. Buddha nature is not mysterious. It is inconceivably wondrous. It is radiant, majestic, subtle, yet clear. It cannot be satisfactorily described in words, ideas, and concepts.

"The dharma in which nothing can be obtained" means that it is not possible to possess anything. We cannot step outside to take hold of it. We already contain everything. To possess something, to obtain something, means to separate oneself from something. From the point of view of realization, everything is unobtainable, including the Buddha Way. That is why we chant in the Four Great Bodhisattva Vows, "The Buddha Way is unattainable. I vow to attain it." We already are the Buddha Way. All of our machinations, grabbing, controlling, and dominating; all of our squabbling and struggling to get, to hoard, to take, is an upside-down way of understanding the nature of the universe and the nature of the self. Be giving. Do not steal.

We cannot live in harmony with the ten thousand things if we constantly play with the illusions of taking and stealing. Dogen's teaching on this precept goes, "When mind and objects are not discriminated, the gate of liberation is open." The "mind" means the self. "Objects" mean the ten thousand things. "Not discriminated" means to experience them as one reality. When you experience them as one reality, the gate to liberation is open. That is realization.

Again, we need to understand this precept not only from the one-mind point of view but also from the literal point of view. Do not steal means anything, anytime, anyplace. Constantly let go. Do not grasp.

Sometimes, out of reverence for life and compassion, it is necessary to steal. In a sense, every time I steal away from you something that you are holding on to, I am violating this precept. But from the point of view of compassion and reverence for life, I am maintaining the very same precept. One student might appreciate that the teacher is functioning as a thief, taking away everything that is precious to him or her, and bow in gratitude. Another student might get very angry in exactly the same setting. Either way, karma is still being created. Karma does not differentiate between good and bad. Karma is the force to propagate itself and continue. "Good and bad" are the dualistic reference frame that we apply to it.

Third Grave Precept

Honor the body. Do not misuse sexuality.

Misusing sexuality indicates the presence of self-centeredness. There is no regard for anything or anyone else. Keep in mind that these precepts arise in the realm of no-self but are designed to function in the world of dualities. Essentially, there is no separation, but we interact within a matrix of time and space where there is separation. You and I are the same thing, but I am not you and you are not me. Both of these configurations and expressions of reality are functioning simultaneously.

This precept is not a rule that prohibits sexuality. It is a rule that admonishes boorish and manipulative sexuality, where sexuality is used solely for one's own pleasure and benefits, with total disregard for the other person. Sometimes that is blatantly obvious, as in the case of rape, purchasing sexual favors, or child abuse, but sometimes it is considerably more subtle and equally devastating. When we use sexuality to control people, even without any physical contact, when we flirt in order to get the things that we want, to satisfy our own desires, we violate this precept.

Bodhidharma said, "Self-nature is inconceivably wondrous. In the dharma where there is nothing to grasp, nothing to take hold of, 'not giving rise to attachment' is called the precept of refraining from misusing sexuality." Everything in this whole universe is characterized by interdependent co-origination. Is there a way to grab on to anything, to hold and control it? Yet we constantly struggle with likes and dislikes. Dogen said, "When the three wheels are pure and clean, nothing is desired. Go the same way as the Buddha."

The three wheels are body, thought, and words, or greed, anger, and ignorance, and refer to the karmic activity of the body. Sexuality involves activity of body, words, and thoughts. All are fundamentally empty. That is the ultimate nature of reality. Yet we are blinded by illusory, dualistic views that give rise to the persistent emotions of love and hate, clinging and rejection, all of which you can call desire. It is all like a dream.

When one clearly verifies for oneself the nature of the self and the nature of all things, then the dualistic distinction begins to dissolve, and love takes on a whole different meaning, one of no separation. Then the loving and sexual relationship between two consenting and caring people is the dharma of unsurpassed enlightenment. It becomes a wonderful expression, not only of human existence, but of the Buddhadharma itself. And it is one and the same as the way of all Buddhas—the activity of Buddha, the movement of Buddha, the expression of Buddha.

Fourth Grave Precept
Manifest truth. Do not lie.

Master Dogen taught, "The dharma wheel unceasingly turns, and there is neither excess nor is there lack. Sweet dew permeates the universe. Gain the essence and realize the truth." Bodhidharma expounded, "Self-nature is inconceivably wondrous and the dharma is beyond all expression. Not speaking even a single word is called the precept of refraining from telling lies."

Self-nature cannot be described with words. No matter how hard we try to explain it, we speak a falsehood. How could we possibly explain it? No matter how many times we say the word bitter, things do not become bitter. No matter how many times we say the word fire, things do not become hot. The word is very different from what it depicts. The word is an abstraction of the reality. It is for that reason that it cannot be explained. It is for that reason that it is inconceivably wondrous. And so it is said of the Buddha that in forty-seven years of teaching he did not utter a single word. Everything is this inconceivably wondrous self-nature.

We tend to look at truth as one side and lies as the other side. We see two distinct polarities. Or we elevate truth to some sort of absolute constant, as if there were a reference book of truth somewhere in the heavens and all things could be checked against it. What is true and what is false? There are no such bottom line certainties. Truth and falsity always exist within a specific framework. Our ways of seeing are very different. What is true for one person is false for another.

"The dharma wheel unceasingly turns, and there is neither excess nor lack. Sweet dew permeates the universe." "Sweet dew" is perfection. The dharma wheel is the teachings of the Buddha, and those teachings of the Buddha tend to go beyond our dualistic perceptions of the universe. The wheel of the Buddha's teachings turns endlessly. It was turning before there was a universe, before the aeon of emptiness. It will continue turning after all the galaxies burn into cosmic dust. It revolves through all the stages of creation and destruction. In the spring, a hundred thousand beautiful flowers. In the fall, the blaze of leaves on ten thousand mountains. We laugh, we cry, we get angry, we stumble, we fall. This is the clear speaking, present at all times and in all places. In this expression, there is no excess and no lack, only completeness of perfection. It is like the sweet rain falling outside the window. It saturates everything.

In each and every thing there is nothing but truth. And yet it is possible, in the realm of this and that, to express falsehood. Usually when we are expressing falsehood, we are protecting ourselves. When this is a self-centered action, it immediately violates this precept, because the precepts spring from no-self.

Under certain circumstances, if you tell the truth, you are violating the precepts. Someone is critically injured in an auto accident, gasping for breath, asking, "Will I be all right?" If you say, "No, you are going to die," that person may give up right there. If you say, "You are doing fine," it may be a lie, but it provides hope for a person to work with. Out of reverence for life and compassion, sometimes we lie. But if that lie is to protect ourself, we violate the precept. From the literal point of view, any lie violates the precept, no matter who it is helping.

But what is the truth? Is it good or is it bad? It depends on where you sit. It depends on your position. It depends on your reference system, your matrix. From the absolute point of view, to even give rise to the thought that there is such a thing as truth

or falsity violates the precept. That is what Bodhidharma meant when he said, "Not speaking even a single word is called the precept of refraining from telling lies." An old master once said, "Shakyamuni Buddha, Ananda, and Amidabutsu—the more they lie, the more they are Buddhas. If they spoke the truth, they would be just ordinary people. But if anyone said that the truth and falsehood are two separate things, this is also deluded speech." These are two parts of the same reality; one cannot exist without the other.

Fifth Grave Precept
Proceed clearly. Do not cloud the mind.

" 'It' has never been. Do not be defiled. 'It' is indeed the great clarity." That is Dogen's teaching. Bodhidharma said, "Self-nature is inconceivably wondrous. In the intrinsically pure dharma, not allowing the mind to become dark is called the precept of refraining from using intoxicants." Instead of stating, "Refrain from using intoxicants," we say, "Proceed clearly. Do not cloud the mind." It is a broader statement. How do we cloud the mind? There are many ways.

We live at a time and in a culture where there are multimillion-dollar industries dedicated to the research and creation of products and pastimes solely for the purpose of anesthetizing us from our lives. We do it not only with alcohol but also with drugs. We do it with heroin, crack, and psychedelics. People say, "Don't you do it with coffee and cigarettes, too?" Of course. But there is an enormous difference between taking a puff on a cigarette and filling your lungs with crack. By blurring that distinction and seeing all substances as homogeneous in their effects, we create excuses and justifications for abuse and for interpreting the precepts to our liking and for our convenience.

During the seventies, when Zen first came to America, everybody was getting stoned on "grass" and tripping on psychedelics. For some adventurous users it was a rush to drop acid and to go sit at the local Zen center. Very soon, people were confusing tripping and *samadhi*. Yet the difference between tripping and samadhi is staggering. Trying to do zazen while you are stoned or drunk is like trying to swim the English Channel with an anchor tied around your neck. It cannot be done. The drugs do precisely the opposite of what samadhi does. Samadhi is a single-pointed awareness and the falling away of body and mind. Pot activates and scatters the mind. Psychedelics plaster it up against the wall. There is no connection whatsoever between those drugs and genuine spiritual practice.

The Buddha said that it is wrong to cloud the mind. Ignorance means to not understand the nature of the self. Ignorance means no light. Drugs and alcohol numb or hyperexcite the mind and extinguish the inherent light that is there. We see through eyes that are blinded by selfishness, self-centeredness, and chemical confusion.

Traditionally, this precept said, "Do not introduce intoxicants. Do not make others defile themselves. This is the great awareness." In other words, do not enable others to introduce intoxicants, thereby defiling themselves. "Do not come bearing liquor." If liquor is not introduced, it cannot be consumed.

Buying is imbibing. Selling is causing others to drink. We need to understand it that way. People get very technical and say, "Well, this is a gift, so I will drink it. I did not buy it. I am not selling it." We do that all the time, stepping over the spirit of the precepts. We know what their intention is, but we prefer to finagle it according to our own preconceived notions. There are a number of monastics and teachers who drink to obvious excess. They justify their drinking by professing that only in the Hinayana tradition does the precept prohibit drinking liquor. They inter-

pret this precept in the Mahayana tradition as not en-
couraging anybody else to drink. Well, that misses it.

There are all kinds of intoxicants. How we understand ourself—all of our ideas based on the dualism
of self and other—can be considered intoxicants.
They cause the greatest darkness. From the absolute
point of view, of course, there is no dualism. There
isn't any way to cloud the mind. But in the realm of
difference and functioning in the world, there surely
is. Just look at the number of deaths caused by people
driving while intoxicated.

Sixth Grave Precept
*See the perfection. Do not speak of others'
errors and faults.*

In his teachings, Master Dogen points out, "In the
midst of the Buddhadharma, we are the same Way,
the same dharma, the same realization, and the same
practice. Do not speak of others' errors and faults.
Do not destroy the Way." How incredibly true that
statement is. Ultimately, you cannot destroy the Way.
It has always been here. It will always be here. It
reaches everywhere. It cannot be created or de-
stroyed. And yet when we attack each other, causing

conflict and turmoil, we cloud the beauty of this life. We cover it with opinions and veil it with confusion.

Bodhidharma taught, "Self-nature is inconceivably wondrous. In the faultless dharma, not speaking of others' faults is called the precept of refraining from speaking of others' errors and faults." The whole universe is this wondrous self-nature. Not a particle is outside of it. It is the true self, the original, bare form of all sentient beings.

Nevertheless, out of reverence for life and compassion, sometimes it is necessary to speak of someone's errors and faults. When you witness a murder and the investigators ask, "Did you see anything?" If you say, "No, I did not. I don't want to speak of anybody's transgressions and imperfections," that violates the precept of not speaking of others' errors and faults.

If you speak of others to inflate and elevate your sense of self, you break this precept. To point out what is wrong with someone else is to place the person below you and create separation. But from the absolute point of view, who is the other? Where is the other? This very body and mind fills the universe. There is no outside, nor other.

In the old days within some spiritual communities, there was an internal rule of not discussing the problems of sangha members with anyone outside the community. Such an attitude, frequently fueled by fear, tended to be a whitewash, a conspiracy of silence. When people were abusing power and hurting others, everybody looked the other way. That is enabling and hypocritical. It is not taking responsibility for the precepts in one's life. But at the same time, there are skillful as well as damaging ways of doing what needs to be done. Attaining the clarity to appreciate that difference and acting accordingly are the key to harmony.

If even the slightest thought of self and other enters into the action, you violate the precept. To speak of others' errors and faults in any way violates the precept. When necessary, speak of others' errors and faults, not to serve the self, but only for the good of others. And then, finally, to even give rise to the thought that there is a self and an other is the most deluded view of all, and it violates this precept. So, "In the midst of the Buddhadharma, we are the same Way, the same dharma, the same realization, and the same practice," for all sentient beings.

Seventh Grave Precept

Realize self and other as one. Do not elevate
the self and blame others.

This precept addresses the importance of taking responsibility and the futility of blaming. When you realize in your life that cause and effect are one, you realize that what you do and what happens to you are really the same thing. To see this clearly is to realize that each one of us is responsible not only for ourselves and our lives but also for the whole phenomenal universe. Whatever happens to this great earth, this universe and its inhabitants, happens to each one of us. It is the same karma. When you realize that, there is no way to avoid taking responsibility for your life. There is no way to blame. There is no way to say, "He made me angry," because you realize that only "you" can make "you" angry. With that realization comes the empowerment to do something about anger.

Master Dogen's teachings on this precept read as follows: "Buddhas and ancestors realize the absolute emptiness and realize the earth. When the great body is manifested, there is neither outside nor inside. When the dharma body is manifested, there is not even a single square inch of earth upon which to stand."

The great body is the body of all sentient beings. It includes the earth and the heavens and the stars and the planets. It contains the whole universe. Because there's nothing outside of it, there's no place to put this gigantic body. What you do to the universe, you

do to yourself. What you do to others, you do to yourself.

Bodhidharma said, "Self-nature is clear and it is obvious in the sphere of equal dharma; not making any distinction between oneself and others is called the precept of refraining from elevating the self and blaming others. To even give rise to the notion that there is someone to blame violates the precept. Self-nature is inconceivably wondrous. In the undifferentiated dharma, not speaking of self and other is called the precept of not elevating the self and blaming others."

The minute you give rise to the notion of a self, you immediately exclude everything else. I always ask the question, "What is the self?" And I always get the same answer, because there is no other way to respond to it. People say, "It's my body, my thoughts, my memory, my history, my ideas." Clearly, all of those are aggregates of the self. What is the self itself? What is a chair? The answer is "legs, arms, back, seat." Those are the aggregates. What's chairness, roomness, treeness? What remains when you remove the aggregates?

There are philosophies that say that when you take away the aggregates, what remains is an essence. There is an essence of a chair. Take away the aggregates and the essence is still there. There is an essence of a room, a tree, a deer. And there is an essence of a self. The essence of the self according to Western philosophy is what we call the soul, *atman*. The experience of Buddhists—thousands of them, men and women for twenty-five hundred years—has been that when you go beyond the aggregates, what remains is nothing—*anatman*, no-self. There never was a self to begin with. It was an idea all along. And it is that idea, that notion of a self, that the Buddha says is the cause of suffering, because you close out everything else. You close out the whole universe. The minute you say, "This bag of skin is me; everything inside it is me and everything outside it is the rest of the universe," you have excluded the whole universe from yourself. And everything you need is out there, and differentiation begins. The ego develops and you need to protect that bag of skin. All sorts of things come up—fear and anxiety, separateness, dualities.

This is why we return repeatedly to Master Dogen's teaching: "To study the Buddha Way is to study the self. To study the self is to forget the self. To forget the self is to be enlightened by the ten thousand things." That is, the whole phenomenal universe. How do you forget the self? Zazen. That statement of Dogen's could be reworded to say: To study the Buddha Way is to study the self. To study the self is to forget the self. And to forget the self is zazen.

What is it that remains when the self is forgotten? People worry about that. Will I be the same? Will I like the same things? Will my friends recognize me? Of course! All you are letting go of is an idea. What is it that remains when the self is forgotten? Everything. The whole universe remains. The only difference is that there is no longer a notion that separates you from it. That simple fact changes the way we perceive ourself and the universe, and it changes the way we relate to the universe. In a sense, the process of zazen is the process of swallowing the universe.

In his instructions to the chief cook, Dogen wrote: "Fools look at themselves as if looking at another. Realized persons look at others and see themselves. The oneness of self and other is the reality realized by Buddhas. The absence of self and other is the reality realized by Buddhas." We can say either all self or all other. It's the same thing. I tell people who are working on the koan Mu to work on it that way: either give yourself up to Mu completely or take Mu and make it yourself. Either way it's the same thing. The only way to see Mu is to be Mu.

Master Dogen continued: "The Buddhas and ancestors have realized the emptiness of the vast sky and the great earth. When they manifest as the great body, they are like the sky without inside or outside. When they manifest as the Dharmakaya there is not even an inch of earth on which to lay hold." There are three *kayas*—bodies of the Buddha, Dharmakaya, Sambhogakaya, and Nirmanakaya. The Dharmakaya is the absolute body of the Buddha; Sambhogakaya is the body of bliss, and Nirmanakaya is the manifestation of the Buddha in the world. All three bodies, all three kayas, are the body of all sentient beings, your body and my body. What we realize is that there are no gaps between self and other.

The emperor once asked the national teacher: "Is there anything I can do for you after your death?" And the national teacher said, "Yes, build me a seamless pagoda." No edges, no gaps. That is the pure Dharmakaya, nothing else. Make for me the pure Dharmakaya with your own body and mind, merge with this great earth and the universe—this is what the national teacher was asking for as his memorial. That seamless pagoda is Mu encompassing the whole universe—isn't it, after all, the complete and total self? Is there room there to elevate oneself and blame others?

We can't practice this precept by supressing the desire to elevate the self and put down others. We can't practice it by trying to praise others. That, too, accomplishes nothing but separation. This precept is about the unity of self and other. It is about seeing the possibility of realizing that unity. Concealing or transforming deluded thoughts concerning self and other does not reach it. The person who seems to be an adversary, making our life miserable, is nobody but ourself. The stress we experience in our life is not coming from someplace else; we create it. The sooner we realize that, the sooner we are able to do something about it.

Eighth Grave Precept
Give generously. Do not be withholding.

There are many ways of giving generously. This precept is not just about giving money or material possessions. Sometimes giving time and attention, simply being present for another human being or another creature, is the most subtle and effective form of giving—just being there, not saying anything, not asking anything, not teaching, not giving, not receiving. It is an incredibly profound and transformative way of giving. It hinges on knowing when that is the right way to act, trusting the situation to elicit that form of giving.

Sometimes we can give our labor, sometimes our concern, sometimes our love. We give, not because something is going to come back our way or because it is good to give. We give because there is no other choice but to give.

This precept was generally understood as spurring us to refrain from begrudging the dharma treasure, the teachings. In other words, it encouraged us not to withhold the dharma. But what is the dharma? Is love the dharma? Is concern the dharma? Is labor the dharma? Is time the dharma? Of course it is—all of it. What is there outside this incredible dharma?

Bodhidharma's One-Mind Precept says, "Self-nature is inconceivably wondrous. In the all-pervading true dharma, not clinging to one form is called the precept of refraining from begrudging the dharma." We can say that not clinging to one form is the precept of giving generously. The "all-pervading true dharma" means the whole universe. "Not clinging to one form" means not to be seized by neediness or wanting. It means not responding constantly to our persistent refrain of "I need, I need, I need" or "I want, I want, I want."

The myriad of dharmas, between heaven and earth, directly and immediately, are the truth, the inconceivably wondrous self-nature. It is ridiculous to even attempt to be withholding. Withholding what from whom? But if we are caught up in a dream of delusion, of separateness, then we are just a bag of skin, everything else is beyond our reach, and desires and regrets arise all the time. So we suffer.

Master Dogen said, "Let go of it, and you are filled by it." The teaching of this precept says that even one gatha, one phrase of the dharma, is the ten thousand things. One dharma, one realization, is all the Buddhas and ancestors. From the very beginning there has been nothing to withhold. One phrase: "Form is emptiness, emptiness is form," or one gatha: "Gate, gate, paragate, parasamgate," is the whole universe. But a gatha or a single phrase of the dharma is also "Good morning," "Boy, it's cold," "How are you?" That also encompasses the ten thousand things, from morning until night, from night until morning, twenty-four hours a day. It is constantly teaching. One dharma and one realization—it is the same thing. Walking, standing, sitting, lying down, is also one realization. Everything is the fundamental realization of the whole universe in its entirety. It is none other than the Buddhas and ancestors; it is none other than all sentient beings. No one is left out, no thing is left out.

Ninth Grave Precept

Actualize harmony. Do not be angry.

Bodhidharma said, "Self-nature is inconceivably wondrous. In the dharma of no-self, not postulating a self is called the precept of refraining from anger." Not creating an idea of a self completely frees us from anger. You cannot have anger unless there is a self. There is no boundless and omniscient self somewhere in the sky that created the whole universe, and there is no tangible and limited self that inhabits this bag of skin. All of reality is simply infinite dharmas that arise and disappear in accord with the laws of karma. There is not one thing standing against another.

Dogen's teaching on this precept says, "Not proceeding, not retreating, not real, not unreal. There is an ocean of bright clouds, there is an ocean of sublime clouds when there is no anger." Not proceeding, not retreating, not real, not unreal. When we proceed from the assumption that all things have their own being that is separate and distinct from everything else, we progress and we regress. There is truth and there is falsity. We make demands. We want things to be different. We constantly try to influence and change the course of events to fit our own preconceived notions and satisfy our endless desires.

Anger is incredibly debilitating. We come into

practice searching, wanting to take care of our questions and doubts. But we carry into our practice all the baggage that has prevented our life from unfolding harmoniously. The baggage is our entangled conglomeration of ideas and positions that have worked together to cause our suffering. It is the deep-seated conditioning that has stifled us and impinged on the lives of others.

We cover the inherent perfection that is originally there with our self-created notion of separateness. When somebody gets ahead of us in the *dokusan* line or moves ahead of us in their practice, we feel that we lose ground, and we get angry. But if we understand that there is no distinction between the two of us, we immediately return to accord with reality, and there is no anger. Yasutani Roshi said that in getting angry we actually break all of the three dimensions of the precepts—the literal, the compassionate, and the one-mind.

If there is no self, if the action of anger is not self-centered, the energy and the content of what is being communicated becomes entirely different. The shout "Wake up!" heals. It is not for the zendo monitor's benefit. He or she is awake. It is for the guy who is sitting there, nodding off. There is no self-centered anger in that. There is anger at the loss of opportunity

to experience our enlightened nature. It is anger similar to the anger of a mother who scolds her child for running out into the road. It is there for the welfare of the child, not because what the child is doing is going to hurt the mother. Expression of such a concern can have a strong impact. There is compassion in it and it reaches people's hearts. Sometimes it is a way of healing.

Tenth Grave Precept

Experience the intimacy of things. Do not defile the Three Treasures.

The One-Mind Precept says, "Self-nature is inconceivably wondrous. In the one dharma, not giving rise to the dualistic view of sentient beings and Buddhas is called the precept of refraining from reviling the Three Treasures." To give rise to the thought "I'm just an ordinary person" reviles and defiles the Three Treasures and breaks this precept. There are only Buddhas. We tend to build dreams of separateness that eventually become nightmares of alienation and isolation, and then we struggle to awaken from the nightmare we have created. To practice this precept is to wake up: there are only Buddhas.

The Buddha nature is inconceivably wondrous.

Not an atom is left out. Not a particle is outside it. Because there is no outside, there is no inside. Therefore there is no way to defile it. The tenth precept closes the loop. The Sixteen Precepts start off with the Three Treasures and end with the Three Treasures.

Master Dogen's teaching on this precept states, "To expound the dharma with this body is the refuge of the world. Its virtue returns to the ocean of omnipotence. It is inexpressible. Wholeheartedly revere and serve this ocean of true reality." The minute you start talking about it, it is no longer the thing you are talking about.

For me, reviling the Three Treasures also includes creating disharmony in the sangha. The essence of sangha is the virtue of harmony. To introduce disharmony is one of the most serious violations within a community. The only situation in which I can envision expelling somebody from the sangha would be if the person were clearly planting seeds of disharmony. It is the worst kind of defiling of the Three Treasures—the Buddha, the Dharma, and the Sangha. It always, and only, happens when we lock ourselves inside our own ego.

All the precepts are nothing other than the life of no-self. To practice them is to practice the life of no-self. They are specifically designed to function in the world of differences and potential conflicts, in the world of this and that, but they arise from no-self.

In order to practice the precepts, we need to take responsibility for them. To practice the precepts is to be in harmony with our life and with the universe. When Master Dogen said, "Practice and enlightenment are one," he was underlining the fact that zazen, the process undertaken to reach enlightenment, and enlightenment itself are the same thing. They are identical, like form and emptiness. When we sit, we manifest the enlightenment of all Buddhas. In the sitting itself, whether we are realized or not, we actualize wisdom and compassion. The same can be said for the precepts. Buddha and precepts are not two separate things. Precepts are Buddha, Buddha is precepts. Each time we acknowledge that we have drifted off a precept, take responsibility and return to the precept, we are manifesting the wisdom and compassion of the Tathagata.

We are part of the first generation of Western Buddhists, and we carry a special burden that will not be carried by future generations and was not carried by the past generations of practitioners in Japan, China, and Korea. That unique burden is that what we are doing with our practice, all over the West, is not just the realization of ourselves but is also the historical process of the transmission of the Buddhadharma from East to West. What we do, how we practice our lives, how we manifest the Buddhadharma by what we do, tells the whole world about these incredible teachings of the Buddha. It is a tremendous responsibility.

It is because of that responsibility that these precepts are so relevant and valuable in our practice. Their profundity is beyond conception. Their flexibility enables them to fill any vessel that contains them. They are dynamic and alive. They nourish and heal. Please, do not take them lightly. Take them into your heart, and give them life in your life. Whether you have received the precepts formally or not, they are yours when you practice them.

Books by John Daido Loori

Cave of Tigers: Modern Zen Encounters

The dynamic dialogues—traditionally known as "dharma combat"—between John Daido Loori and his students. Culled from formal public meetings over fifteen years, these transcripts convey the excitement and seriousness of practicing on the sharp edge of our self-exploration, with all of its associated rawness, vulnerability, spontaneity, and wonder.

Bringing the Sacred to Life: The Daily Practice of Zen Ritual

What the bows, chants, incense, and altars of Zen are all about. Loori shows how the Zen liturgy is a practice for bringing the energy of enlightenment to everyday life. The book includes instructions for performing the Zen home liturgy, as practiced in the Mountains and Rivers Order, as well as all the principal daily chants.

Hearing with the Eye: Photographs from Point Lobos

John Daido Loori's stunning array of images taken at Point Lobos, California beautifully complements his commentary of Master Dogen's *Teachings of the Insentient*, a profound exploration of the mystical reality of the insentient. The words and images presented in this book are an attempt to enter the hidden universe of the insentient and see "things for what else they are." They are an invitation to discover the full spectrum of the teachings of rocks, mountains, rivers, and trees.

Making Love with Light: Contemplating Nature with Words and Photographs

Brings together Loori's vocation as Zen teacher with his talent as a photographer. The essays, images, and poems on these pages fill the gap that separates us from ourselves, and from all that is wild, free, and uncultivated. They are an expression of love using light. Seventy-five full-color plates with accompanying Zen poems form a panoramic vista of and give voice to the mountains, rivers, rock, and sky.

Mountain Record of Zen Talks

A collection of Loori's talks exploring Zen practice as a spiritual journey of self-discovery: beginning with the development of a sound appreciation of zazen, realizing the ground of being and the nature of reality, and actualizing these insights in the activities of the world.

Finding the Still Point: A Beginner's Guide to Zen Meditation

Beginner's instruction in zazen, seated Zen meditation—accompanied with an audio CD that includes a dharma talk and two timed meditation periods.

Teachings of the Earth: Zen and the Environment

A unique exposition of the awakened ecological consciousness implicit in Zen Buddhism—and its resonances with such "non-Zen" figures as Walt Whitman and Henry David Thoreau.

Two Arrows Meeting in Mid-Air: The Zen Koan

The definitive volume to koan study and its relevance for modern practitioners. Presents a comprehensive overview of the history and use of koans in Zen training, and contains formal discourses on twenty-one ancient and modern cases. Clearly demonstrates the transformative power of working with koans.